A GUIDE ON HANDLING ANGER; Phenomenal help guide on how to manage explosive anger issues.

David A. Peters

Copyright

Table of contents

Chapter 1

Anger Equality and causes.

Anger can be powerful if you realize what's emotionally healthy and what's not.

But the chorus of women's objections isn't always welcome — particularly when society believes that they're furious.
For males, fury is regarded as manly. For women, society frequently tells us it's inappropriate.

But societal perceptions that a woman's wrath is poisonous may badly influence our emotional and physical health. Being taught, as a girl, that anger is wrong may cause guilt to accumulate, which can hinder us from expressing this healthy emotion.
While we can't control how others perceive our anger – learning how to recognize, express, and utilize this feeling may be liberating.

If you're getting fired up about a subject, it's far better physically and emotionally to become quiet, and centered, and then channel your ideas and views in a useful, sensible manner, such as participating in real-time in-person discourse.

Anger is the true issue

Mary McNaughton-Cassill, Ph.D., a professor of psychology at the University of Texas in San Antonio, pointed to a 2013 study by trusted Source that reveals persons using websites to rage are more likely to have anger problems in their personal life.

"In general, expressing anger in person by screaming or bashing things, or online ranting, tends to enhance your levels of anger," McNaughton-Cassill told Healthline.

She pointed out that animosity has been related to an increased risk for heart disease.

"This is not to argue that anger is never legitimate, but merely going over and over why you are furious does not lessen emotionality or solve problems," she continued.

McNaughton-Cassill thinks that individuals need to gain media literacy skills to counteract bogus news and propaganda. These abilities may help decrease raving and its adverse health repercussions.

“Especially on social media, we need to be careful about what we publish and share,” she added. “If you merely want to blow off steam, raving may feel nice in the short term, but it doesn’t lessen your anger levels generally and is unlikely to foster meaningful discourse with others.”

Both men and women are frequently embarrassed about their anger, however, it seems they may perceive their anger differently, according to continuing study. For example, gender socialization may alter how men and women control their anger, studies have discovered.

"Both men and women have been ill-served by the gender indoctrination they have received," says psychologist Sandra Thomas, Ph.D., a major researcher in women's anger who has lately also begun examining men's experiences with rage. "Men have been pushed to be more overt with their fury. If [boys] quarrel on the playground, they act it out with their fists. Girls have been instructed to keep their fury down."

Indeed, rage in males is frequently perceived as "masculine"—it is considered as "manly" when men participate in fistfights or act their anger out physically, says Thomas, head of the nursing Ph.D. program at the University of Tennessee, Knoxville. "For women, acting out in that manner is not encouraged," she explains. "Women frequently receive the message that rage is unpleasant and unfeminine." Therefore, their anger may be channeled in passive-aggressive methods such as pouting or harmful gossip, she explains.

In her perspective, however, neither method in its extreme is healthy. It is crucial, Thomas argues, for both boys and girls to be upfront and straightforward when they are upset and to employ problem-solving skills in coping with their anger.

"Things are not getting better in angry behavior," adds Thomas, who highlights the numerous incidents nowadays of violence among minors. "We need to understand what anger is about before we can act successfully."

Differences in anger expression

Also essential, experts argue, are efforts to eliminate gender prejudices about rage. June Tangney, Ph.D., for example, has called into question prevalent preconceptions about women and anger, such as the idea that women have difficulties with rage. Women don't have a problem with anger—they simply handle it differently, says Tangney, professor of psychology at George Mason University.

Women tend not to be as forceful as males in expressing anger and prefer to speak about their emotions more, she adds. "They are more proactive and employ more problem-solving ways in addressing a topic with a person they are furious with," adds Tangney.

And what makes average women furious day-to-day? In 1993, Thomas performed the Women's Anger Study, a large-scale survey including 535 women between the ages of 25 and 66. The research identified three common bases of women's anger: helplessness, unfairness, and the irresponsibility of other people.

While the study has not yet revealed that distinct variables drive men's anger, researchers continue to identify variances in how men and women perceive it. Such was the case for Raymond DiGiuseppe, Ph.D., head of the psychology department at St. John's University in New York, in his study to design a new rage disorder scale. In a poll of 1,300 adults aged 18 to 90, DiGiuseppe explored 18 subscales of anger, including how individuals perceive their anger, how long the anger lasts, and what they become furious over.

While he discovered that differences between men's and women's overall anger ratings were not significant, he did uncover variations in the way they feel anger. Specifically, males scored higher on physical aggressiveness, passive aggression, and experiences of impulsively coping with their anger. They also more frequently had a vengeance motivation behind their rage and scored higher on coercing other individuals.

Women, on the other hand, were found to feel furious longer, more resentful, and less inclined to communicate their anger, compared with males. DiGuiseppe discovered that women employed indirect violence by "writing off" a larger percentage of people—intending to never talk to them again because of their displeasure.

Anger steadily reduces with age, DiGiuseppe observed, and variations in the areas of anger between the sexes decrease for people older than 50, while males are still more likely to be violent and women are still more likely to experience longer bouts of anger. DiGiuseppe's findings will be published this year by Multi-Health Systems, a Canadian publisher of psychological examinations.

So as a man or woman, you are permitted to be furious but it is recommended to restrict and comprehend where that emotion is bringing you to.

There are solid answers to it here.
Read on...

As a psychologist, here's what I want both women and men to know about rage.

1. Anger isn't a hazardous emotion
Growing up in households where disagreement was pushed under the rug or expressed violently might teach the attitude that anger is bad.

It's crucial to recognize that anger doesn't injure others.

What's detrimental is how fury is transmitted. Anger that's expressed as physical or verbal violence leaves emotional scars, while irritation that's conveyed non-violently may create connection and help restore relationships.

ANGER IS AN EMOTIONAL TRAFFIC SIGNAL.

It notifies us that we've been mistreated or damaged in some manner. When we don't feel embarrassed about our anger, it may help us realize our needs and foster self-care.

2. Hiding anger has repercussions
Believing that anger is harmful might make us swallow our fury. But concealing this feeling has implications. Prolonged anger is linkedTrusted Source to health difficulties including sleeplessness, anxiety, and depression.

Unresolved and unexpressed anger may also lead to harmful habits, such as drug use, overeating, and over-spending.

Uncomfortable emotions need to be eased, and when we don't receive loving support, we find alternate methods to numb our feelings.

KEEP YOUR FEELINGS HEALTHY BY EXPRESSING THEM.
Even if it seems hazardous to address the unpleasant person or scenario, activities like writing, singing, meditation, or talking with a therapist may give a cathartic release for displeasure.

3. Anger related to results may be emotionally hazardous
Relying on our anger to modify results may cause us to feel hopeless, depressed, and disillusioned, particularly if the person or circumstance doesn't change.

With that in mind, before addressing someone, ask yourself: "What do I want to achieve from this interaction?" and "How will I feel if nothing changes?"

We can't change other people, and although it may be depressing, it may also be liberating to know what we can and cannot manage.

4. Healthy methods to express rage
Using "I" phrases is one of the finest methods to vocally convey furious sentiments.

Owning your feelings helps lessen the other person's barriers, enabling them to hear and accept your remarks. Instead of stating, "You constantly irritate me," try adding, "I'm upset because..."

If addressing the individual isn't viable, putting your energy into action may create a feeling of solidarity, which can be encouraging and restorative.

In circumstances when individuals have endured trauma, such as abuse, assault, or the loss of a loved one, knowing that your experience may benefit another person may feel empowered.

Everyone has experienced fury. The degree of your anger might vary from deep displeasure to severe wrath. It's acceptable and good to feel irritated from time to time in reaction to specific events.

But occasionally individuals feel an uncontrolled rage that frequently grows, even when the provocation is mild. In this scenario, rage is not a natural feeling but a severe issue.

What causes rage and anger problems?

Anger arises from a multitude of causes and may vary considerably. Some frequent rage triggers include:

Personal troubles, such as missing a promotion at work or marital difficulties.

The difficulty caused by another person such as canceling plans.
An occurrence like terrible traffic or getting in a vehicle accident
Memories of a painful or enraging event.

In other circumstances, an anger issue may be created by early trauma or experiences in a person's life that has impacted their personality. In other situations, hormonal changes may also produce rage, as can certain mental problems.

What are the signs of an anger problem?
Some symptoms that your rage is not typical include:

Anger impacts your relationships and social life.
Feeling that you have to conceal or keep in your wrath.
Constant negative thinking and dwelling on unfavorable events.
Constantly feeling angry, annoyed, and aggressive.
Arguing with people regularly, and growing angry in the process.
Being physically aggressive when you're enraged.
Threatening harm against individuals or their property.
An inability to manage your rage.

Feeling motivated to do, or doing, aggressive or impulsive activities because you feel furious, such as driving dangerously or damaging items.
Staying away from particular settings because you're scared or upset about your furious outbursts.

What are the diagnostic criteria for an anger problem?
Anger alone doesn't constitute a mental disease, therefore there's no defined diagnosis for anger disorders in the current version of the Diagnostic and Statistical Manual of Mental Disorders (DSM-5) (DSM-5).

However, it identifies more than 32 mental diseases — such as borderline personality disorder and intermittent explosive disorder — that involve rage as a symptom. Your rage issue is likely triggered by an underlying mental disease.

What may happen if an anger issue isn't treated?

If you don't deal with your anger issue, it might one day build to a point where you do something drastic and terrible. Violence is one potential effect. You might become so upset that you wind up injuring yourself or someone you care about without trying to do so.

Chapter 2

Understanding emotional triggers.

Do you struggle to manage your anger in certain situations? Have you ever experienced a moment when your fury appeared to spiral out of control in a couple of seconds?

Perhaps others characterize you as being "too sensitive" or you feel like people know how to press your buttons.
If any of these events ring true, you're undoubtedly experiencing your emotional triggers.

What are rage triggers?
Anger triggers are like any emotional trigger. It's a sensitive place in your emotions that gets stirred up by a given scenario, person, issue, etc.
No need to fear. We all have emotional triggers. Different events might evoke different feelings for everyone. So what produces these distinct triggers? Your life experience makes the difference. The stuff you encounter in life educates your brain to behave in specific ways.

The things that may spark an emotion are practically unlimited. It might be a specific word, an action, a location, or a person, the list truly could continue. It's everything that your brain identifies with a specific recollection of your life experience.

The problematic thing with triggers is that you may not be aware of them. As a Denver anger management counselor, I frequently hear comments such as "I simply lose control of my anger, but I don't know why." In these instances, your emotions are being activated without your knowledge.
Some of your triggers could be evident. You probably know that if your wife looks at you a specific way you might feel incredibly irritated. Perhaps your kids do something in particular that might set you off.

The first thing you have to do to modify an anger trigger is to recognize what is setting you off. During anger management therapy you will learn how to identify and become more aware of your anger triggers.

Awareness is the cornerstone for providing excellent treatment. One of the great features of therapy is bringing things into your consciousness so that you may modify how they affect your life.

Becoming aware of your anger triggers provides you the ability to regulate your own emotions.

Dealing with rage triggers

Once you become more aware of what's driving your anger you may begin to heal. Often rage triggers are a consequence of emotional suffering. The work you will have to undertake will depend upon the trigger.

For example, your wrath can be aroused by your spouse. In this scenario, you will probably need to analyze how resentment is harming your relationship. In this case, you will need to focus on forgiveness to shift your anger trigger.

Often rage triggers involve going through some bad or painful events in your life. Common traumatic events associated with rage include things such as enduring abuse as a kid, being assaulted by someone, or a circumstance when your physical safety was at risk.

Working through anything such as a terrible incident or life experience could need some extra treatment from a mental health specialist. If you discover that you simply can't seem to manage your anger, you may contact a trained therapist in your region.

Take Control of Your Anger.

Chapter 3

Communicate.

When individuals feel furious, they tend to leap to conclusions, which might be wrong. When you're having a heated fight, calm down and think through your comments before lashing out. Remember to listen to the other person in the discussion. Good communication may help you settle issues before your anger rises.

How can a medical professional help you handle anger?
A medical practitioner such as a psychiatrist or psychologist might propose strategies to regulate your anger. Talk therapy may be useful, as can anger control programs.

Anger management programs may be taken in person or online. They may also be studied in a book. Anger management will teach you how to recognize your frustrations early on and then address them. This may require telling people, or yourself, what you need, but also being calm and in command of the situation (as opposed to having an angry outburst) (as opposed to having an angry outburst).

These sessions may be done alone with a counselor or with a counselor accompanied by your partner or a group. The kind, duration, and the number of sessions will depend on the program and your specific requirements. This form of therapy might be quick or may endure for many weeks or months.

When you begin the sessions, your counselor will help you identify your anger triggers and scan your body and emotions for symptoms of anger. Noticing and checking in with these warning indicators is one early step required to help regulate your anger. Later on, you'll discover behavioral strategies and ways of thinking that will help you manage your anger. If you have underlying mental health concerns, your counselor will also help you manage them, frequently making it simpler to regulate your anger.

What is the prognosis for an anger problem?
Anger doesn't have to come in the way of you enjoying a happy, complete life. If you're feeling excessive rage, visit your physician or mental healthcare practitioner. They will assist you to discover which professional treatments may be able to help you manage.

What's more, there are various methods you may learn to regulate your anger at home. With time and a continuous effort, you'll be able to more easily regulate your anger and enhance your quality of life.

And they're not only providing positive opinions in online product or service evaluations.

Social media is flooded with rants and raves about everything.

"People feel freer to speak out online," Shoshana Bennett, Ph.D., a California-based psychotherapist told Healthline. "It's much simpler to yell without an audience gazing at you in person. It's more comfortable to unload since you're disguised behind a screen."

Blowing off anger online may seem therapeutic for the author in the short term.

However, specialists warn raving may cause long-term health implications for both the ranter and the reader.

Bennett feels that internet outbursts are never good. She claimed her clients report being more agitated after raving themselves or reading someone else's outburst.

"As a psychologist, I know how emotionally damaging it can be," Bennett added. "I'll guess that if tested, cortisol blood levels would be found high in the ranter. And as we well know, elevated cortisol daily may create all sorts of physical health issues."

Another difficulty with internet tirades is that they remain online forever.

So if you alter your mind, it might be a cause of further worry, Bennett added.

Ranting may be excellent for our health whether we're chatting to a buddy in person or on the phone. It might be cathartic to sound off, Bennett remarked.

"The difference is that in real-time with a support person who is there, listening, and providing you feedback when wanted, there can be more of a sensible discourse and working out of emotions. Instead of simply negatively spouting off, it may turn into something positive," she remarked.

Communicate more when you feel you should vent about a specific injustice you feel or perceive. It may curb a lot of unforeseen issues or those to come.

Chapter 4

Tools to promote emotional regulation.

What is emotional regulation disorder?
An emotional regulation disorder is a condition where someone has trouble regulating their emotions. This failure to effectively control emotions is referred to as dysregulation. Dysregulation is a poor capacity to moderate emotional responses or maintain emotions within an acceptable range.

A person with an emotional regulation disorder is more prone to suffer significant swings in mood. These oscillations in turn adversely affect the person's behavior.

The emotional regulation problem may occur in some of the following:

Difficulty forming and maintaining strong connections
Self-destructive conduct
Hypersensitivity
Frequent meltdowns or temper outbursts

Outbursts of emotions that are projected onto someone who did not cause the injury

Emotional control problems may often accompany other mental health disorders. Disorders such as depression, stress, or borderline personality disorder sometimes affect emotional control.

Emotions are a common component of daily existence. We feel annoyed when we're stopped in traffic. We feel melancholy when we miss our loved ones. We might become furious when someone lets us down or does something to harm us.

While we expect to feel these emotions consistently, some individuals start to experience more turbulent emotions. They experience higher highs and lower lows, and these peaks and troughs begin to affect their life. Individuals who experience extreme emotions may find themselves peaceful one minute and then unhappy or furious the next.

While many of us might have periods when our emotions spin out of control, for some individuals it occurs constantly. Their fast-shifting emotions might force them to do and say things they subsequently regret. They may ruin relationships or undermine their credibility with others.

There might be a lot of reasons when someone loses control of their emotions. They may be genetically susceptible to these quick alterations. They may never have seen healthy emotional control modeled or mastered the techniques. They may lose control when they face triggers from terrible experiences that transpired in the past. There might also be physical changes that lead a person to lose control of their emotions, such as tiredness or a dip in blood sugar.

No of the cause for the emotional instability, the good news is that we can develop greater self-regulation. We can all benefit from learning ways to manage our emotions. Emotional regulation is the capacity to better manage our emotional state.

What are emotional control and regulation?

Emotional control and regulation are doing any action that modifies the intensity of an emotional experience. It doesn't imply concealing or ignoring feelings. With emotional management abilities, you can control which feelings you experience as well as how you exhibit them.

Ultimately, it relates to the capacity to successfully exercise control over our emotions using a broad number of ways.

Some individuals are better at managing their emotions than others. They are strong in emotional intelligence and are aware of both their sensations and the sentiments of others. While it may appear like they're simply "naturally tranquil," some folks experience unpleasant sensations too. They've simply discovered coping techniques that enable them to self-regulate tough emotions.

The good news is that emotional self-regulation isn’t a static quality. Emotion management abilities may be learned and developed through time. Learning how to handle unfavorable situations may help your mental and physical health.

Why is emotional management important?
As growing up adolescents, we are expected to regulate our emotions in ways that are socially acceptable and assist us to navigate our lives. When our emotions get the better of us, they may create issues.

Many circumstances may impair emotional control. These include our ideas about unpleasant feelings or a lack of emotional management abilities. Sometimes, difficult events might produce exceptionally intense feelings.

One of the ways that emotional volatility may affect us involves the influence it might have on our relationships with others. For example, when we cannot appropriately manage our anger, we are prone to say things that hurt others around us and lead them to draw away. We may regret the things we've spoken about or have to spend effort healing connections.

In addition to having a detrimental influence on our relationships, an inability to manage our emotions may also injure us. Feeling extreme melancholy may diminish well-being and create unneeded pain. Living with undiluted dread might stand in the way of our capacity to take chances and have new life experiences.

5 emotion regulating abilities you should learn.
There are a variety of abilities that may help us self-regulate our emotions.

1. Create space

Emotions happen swiftly. We don't think "now I will be angry" – we are simply instantly clench-jawed and enraged. So the number one skill in controlling tough emotions, the gift we can offer ourselves, is to halt. Take a breath. Slow down the moment between trigger and reaction.

2. Noticing what you feel

An equally vital skill is the capacity to become aware of what you're experiencing. Dr. Judson Brewer, MD Ph.D. advises methods for being more interested in your bodily responses. Tune in to yourself and consider: in what places of your body are you detecting sensations? Is your stomach upset? Is your heart racing? Do you feel stress in your neck or head?

Your physical symptoms might be indicators of what you are feeling emotional. Inquiring into what is happening to you physically might also divert your concentration and enable some of the intensity of the feeling to fade away.

3. Naming what you feel

After realizing what you feel, the capacity to identify it might help you acquire control of what is occurring. Ask yourself: what would you label the feelings you're feeling? Is it anger, sorrow, disappointment, or resentment? What else is it? One powerful emotion that sometimes lurks behind others is dread.

Many of us experience more than one emotion at a time, so don't hesitate to name several emotions you could be experiencing. Then delve a bit deeper. If you sense fear, what are you terrified of? If you experience rage, what are you furious about or toward? Being able to identify your feelings can help you go one step closer to communicating your emotions with others.

4. Accepting the feeling

Emotions are a normal and natural aspect of how we react to events. Rather than beating yourself up for feeling furious or terrified, acknowledge that your emotional responses are legitimate. Try to exercise self-compassion and give yourself grace. Recognize that having emotions is typical human behavior.

5. Practicing mindfulness

Mindfulness helps us "live in the moment" by paying attention to what is within us. Use your senses to observe what is occurring around you in nonjudgmental ways. These strategies may help you keep calm and avoid participating in negative thinking patterns while you are in the middle of emotional discomfort.

Chapter 5

7 strategies that can help you regulate your emotions.

There are a lot of emotion control tactics that individuals may practice to increase their coping abilities. It is necessary to assess which methods are most beneficial and which ones to avoid.

There are two major kinds of emotional regulation. The first is reappraisal: modifying how we think about something to change our reaction. The second is suppression, which is connected to more unfavorable effects. Research reveals that neglecting our emotions is related to unhappiness and low well-being.

Let's look at 7 tactics that might assist you to control emotions healthily and beneficially.

1. Identify and minimize triggers

You shouldn't strive to avoid bad feelings – or be scared of them. But you also don't have to keep placing yourself in a position that brings on bad feelings. Start to search for patterns or elements that are present when you start to experience powerful emotions. This demands some inquiry and honesty. Did anything make you feel small? Strong emotions typically rise out of our deep-seated anxieties, particularly the ones we conceal. What is occurring around you and what old experiences does it bring up for you?

When you identify these triggers, you may start to analyze why they carry so much weight and if you can minimize their relevance. For example, a CEO could be reluctant to disclose that he gets upset when talking numbers since he suffered in math class. Understanding this trigger could be enough. Or, the CEO can prefer to examine the monthly charts in private to avoid the trigger of feeling that everyone else is waiting for him.

2. Tune into physical symptoms

Pay attention to how you are feeling, particularly if you are feeling hungry or weary. These variables might intensify your emotions and lead you to perceive your feelings more intensely. If you can treat the underlying problem (e.g. hunger, weariness), you can adjust your emotional reaction.

3. Consider the tale you are telling yourself

In the lack of information, we fill in the spaces with details of our own. Perhaps you are feeling rejected because you haven't heard from a family member; you assume it is because they no longer care about you.

Before you make these attributions, ask yourself: what alternative explanations could be possible? In the case of the family member, what else may be going on with them that would hinder them from reaching out to you? Could they be busy or sick? Are they well-intentioned person who frequently forgets to follow through on commitments?

BetterUp's Shonna Waters advocates the "just like me" strategy. Whatever reason or action you are giving to the other person (there's nearly always another person involved), add "just like me" to the end. It is a means of reminding oneself that they are also flawed human beings.

4. Engage in positive self-talk

When our emotions seem overpowering, our self-talk might turn negative: "I screwed up again" or "everyone else is so awful." If you treat yourself with empathy, you can replace some of this negative discourse with good remarks. Try motivating yourself by stating "I always try so hard" or "People are doing the best they can." This adjustment may assist lessen the feelings we're experiencing. You might still feel unhappy with a scenario that isn't functioning but no longer has to assign blame or generalize it beyond the context.

5. Decide how to react

In most circumstances, we have an option regarding how to react. If you tend to react to emotions of anger by lashing out at others, you certainly see the detrimental effect it is having on your relationships. You could also realize that it doesn't feel well. Or, it feels fantastic at the time, but the repercussions are awful.

Next time you experience anger or fear, understand that you get to choose how you want to react. That acknowledgment is tremendous. Rather than lashing out, might you attempt an alternative response? Is it feasible for you to inform someone that you're feeling upset rather than speaking brutally to them? Get inquisitive about what will happen if you mix up your replies. How did you feel? How did the other person respond?

6. Look for good feelings

Human humans naturally assign greater weight to negative emotions than pleasant ones. This is known as negative bias. Negative emotions, including contempt, rage, and grief tend to carry a lot of weight. Positive sentiments, such as satisfaction, interest, and thankfulness are quieter. Making a practice of identifying these pleasant events helps promote resilience and well-being.

7. Seek out a therapist

Managing our own emotions might be tricky. It takes a great degree of self-awareness. When we're having a hard time, our emotional self-regulation starts to deteriorate. Sometimes we need a partner like a therapist who can assist us gain stronger self-regulation abilities. Fortunately, there are a variety of therapeutic options that may help us learn to better manage our emotions.

Chapter 6

Conclusion.

How can you handle your anger at home?

There are various effective strategies to moderate your anger at home.

Relaxation techniques
These include breathing deeply and envisioning relaxing scenes in your thoughts. When trying to relax, breathe from deep within your lungs, inhaling and expelling slowly in a controlled way. Repeat a relaxing word or phrase, such as “relax” or “take it easy.”

You may also choose to envision a soothing experience, either from your recollection or imagination. Slow, yoga-like motions may also help relax your body and make you feel calmer.

Cognitive restructuring
Changing the way you think can influence the way you express your anger. When a person is furious, it’s generally easy for them to think drastically. It’s

crucial to focus on communicating sensible, rather than irrational, opinions.

Avoid using the terms “always” and “never” in your thoughts and speech. Such terms are wrong and can make you feel like your anger is justified, which makes it worse. These remarks can also hurt others who may be attempting to help you solve your dilemma.

Problem-solving

Anger can be caused by very real situations. While some anger is warranted when things don’t go as planned, it’s not the fury that will help you fix the situation. The best way to approach a situation that’s making you upset is to not focus on the solution but to figure out how to fix the problem.

You can achieve that by developing a plan and checking in with it often so that you can verify your progress often. Don’t be irritated if the manner the problem ends up getting fixed isn’t exactly the way you planned. Just make your best effort.

How can you handle your anger at home?

There are various effective strategies to moderate your anger at home.

Relaxation techniques

These include breathing deeply and envisioning relaxing scenes in your thoughts. When trying to relax, breathe from deep within your lungs, inhaling and expelling slowly in a controlled way. Repeat a relaxing word or phrase, such as "relax" or "take it easy."

You may also choose to envision a soothing experience, either from your recollection or imagination. Slow, yoga-like motions may also help relax your body and make you feel calmer.

Cognitive restructuring

Changing the way you think can influence the way you express your anger. When a person is furious, it's generally easy for them to think drastically. It's crucial to focus on communicating sensible, rather than irrational, opinions.

Avoid using the terms "always" and "never" in your thoughts and speech. Such terms are wrong and can make you feel like your anger is justified, which makes it worse. These remarks can also hurt others who may be attempting to help you solve your dilemma.

Problem-solving

Anger can be caused by very real situations. While some anger is warranted when things don't go as planned, it's not the fury that will help you fix the situation. The best way to approach a situation that's making you upset is to not focus on the solution but to figure out how to fix the problem.

You can achieve that by developing a plan and checking in with it often so that you can verify your progress often. Don't be irritated if the manner the problem ends up getting fixed isn't exactly the way you planned. Just make your best effort.

www.ingramcontent.com/pod-product-compliance
Lightning Source LLC
LaVergne TN
LVHW020532160826
845677LV00015B/4015
* 9 7 9 8 8 4 7 7 9 7 9 5 5 *